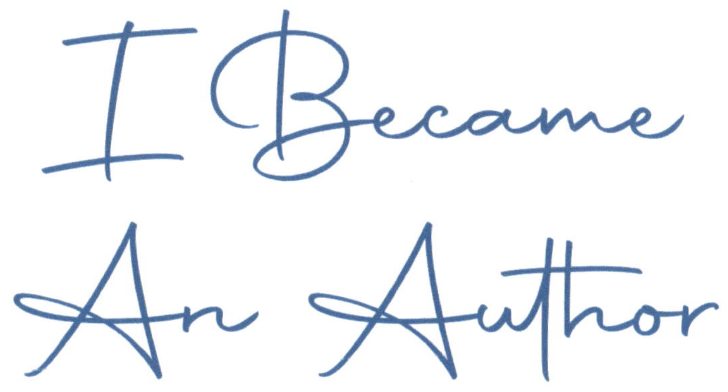

MEDAD AHMED NOUR

ISBN
Hardcase 979-8-89777-353-4
Paperback 979-8-89724-530-7

Contents

Preface

The journey to becoming a young author is filled with moments of doubt, challenge, and discovery. I Became an Author is not just a guide; it is a reflection of my personal, limited experiences and the lessons I have learned along the way. Writing has always been a dream of mine, but it hasn't been without its obstacles. I struggled with unfinished ideas, a limited vocabulary, and the overwhelming feeling of being alone in my pursuit. However, through perseverance and support, I was able to overcome these hurdles and transform my dream into reality.

In the chapters ahead, I will share the challenges I faced, the solutions I found, and the steps that ultimately led me to become an author. Whether you're a young writer or someone preparing to publish your first book, I hope my personal journey can inspire you and offer practical advice to help you navigate your own path to authorship.

Chapter 01

The Beginning of My Writing Journey

1.1   The Clouds Language

I hesitated for a long time before I decided to write my first book. The struggle was real, and it felt like my dream of becoming an author would never come true. It took me more than a year and a half to finish the first draft. Part of the delay was the topic I chose to write about—it was deeply personal and significant for everyone my age, and that made me unsure if I should even share it.

I was born in 2015 in my beloved country, Sudan, and grew up in a warm and loving family. My family consists of my father, my mother, and my older sister, who is four years older than me. Despite the age gap, we were so close that the years between us didn't seem to matter. My sister wasn't just a sibling to me; she was my companion and my best friend. My parents showered us with love and care, not just for us but also for our extended family. This environment helped me grow confident at a very young age.

As I got older and became more aware of the world around me, my social circle began to widen. I started to interact more with my relatives and neighbours, observing how they lived and what they talked about.

The day in December 2022 when my family and I were sitting on the balcony of our apartment in the

Sultanate of Oman is still vivid in my mind. The clouds above us were constantly shifting, forming shapes that seemed almost magical. I watched in awe, and suddenly, an idea struck me: "Why not write a story about this?" The thought excited me. I had never tried writing a story before, but this seemed like the perfect moment to start.

I rushed to my room to grab my phone, eager to capture the clouds before they changed. But by the time I returned, the shapes had disappeared. All that remained was a fleeting memory—an image in my mind that felt so real but seemed impossible to prove to anyone else. How could I show others what I had seen? What if they didn't believe me?

I felt a deep sense of disappointment, and my father, seeing my frustration, kindly suggested, "Why not try drawing it, since you remember it so well?" But I looked at him and said, "It's too difficult. I can't draw what I saw." He smiled and then said, "Well, then the only thing left is to write it down."

That's when I felt completely stuck. Writing... how could I possibly write it? I didn't even know where to begin. I had this idea in my mind, but turning it into words felt impossible. I didn't have the words, and I didn't know how to make sense of everything I had seen. Sitting there, I tried to collect my thoughts, but it was like a cloud of confusion settled in my mind.

The ideas wouldn't come. Each time I thought about writing, I only felt more frustrated. It was a terrible feeling—like being trapped inside a maze without a way out. How could I translate the beauty and mystery of the clouds into words? How could I share something that was so fleeting, so difficult to capture, with others?

When I couldn't think of anything to write, I went to my father, feeling frustrated. I told him that I was stuck and didn't know how to start. He listened patiently, as he always does, and kindly offered to help. He didn't give me the answers right away; instead, he encouraged me to keep thinking and to trust my creativity.

Together, we came up with the idea for a long writing project called *The Cloud's Language*. Inspired by the clouds we had seen earlier, we imagined a story based on their ever-changing shapes and the beauty they represented. It felt like the perfect way to express my feelings and ideas. That moment of collaboration with my father gave me the confidence to start.

From that point on, I couldn't stop writing. One story turned into another, and soon, I found myself writing with excitement, eager to explore my imagination. But then, a new idea came to me, one that felt even more personal. "Why not write my journey about how you became an author?" I thought. This idea sparked something deep inside me. I wanted to share my journey, not only for myself but to help children my age who might face the same struggles in finding their own voice.

I decided to write this advisory story, hoping one day to publish it. My goal was to inspire others, especially kids who might feel just like I did, and help them avoid the obstacles I had to overcome. I wanted to show them that writing could be a powerful tool for self-expression, and that no matter how difficult the path may seem, they could find their way too.

I learned that becoming an author is not just about writing; it's about organising your thoughts, managing your time, and, most importantly, being creative and honest with your feelings and ideas. It felt like a dream when my first book started gaining attention. Soon, people became interested in reading it, and I found myself writing even more stories.

My father had another brilliant idea for my older sister and me to finish our story together and post it on Amazon for a wide audience. This way, we could show how children like us struggled to reach this stage in writing and publishing. If we succeeded, he promised to reward us with money. A friendly competition started between my sister and me, and we both pushed ourselves to be better, as we had so much to express in our first books.

I never imagined that such a simple moment—sitting on a balcony, watching the clouds—would spark the journey that led me to become an author. As we gazed at the sky, each of us saw different shapes in the clouds. One person would say, "That looks like a horse!" and another would argue, "No, it looks like a plane!" The fun in imagining what the clouds resembled was endless, and it was at that moment that my idea began to take shape.

The next day, the idea blossomed into something bigger: a book called *The Language of the Clouds*, where my sister and I would explore the idea of clouds talking to each other, moving, and even crying. We would tell this story through illustrations and narratives for children. We believed this topic was unique and hadn't been done before, which inspired us to dive right into creating the book.

However, things didn't go as smoothly as we expected. We struggled with how to express our ideas in a clear way, and our progress stalled when the second academic term began. Writing a book wasn't as easy as I thought. The skill to write a book is more than just having an idea—it requires talent, patience, and the right tools. Despite the challenges, I continued to practice writing, and through these experiences, I realised that writing isn't just about having an idea. It's about learning how to refine that idea and express it in a way that others can connect with.

From these struggles and attempts, the idea for this book was born: to share my journey, my attempts, and the lessons I learned along the way. Writing this book is not just about my story—it's meant to inspire others, especially those my age, who dream of becoming authors. Through my experiences, I hope to show them that becoming a writer isn't just a goal; it's a journey that takes time, persistence, and a lot of effort. But anyone can do it, just like I did.

I took the photos above myself, and I'm still on track to write another book, this time about the language of clouds. I'm excited to explore how I can dive deeper into this concept and create a beautiful story for kids. Even though I'm a kid myself, I feel like I'm at a different level now, and I can share my understanding in a way that can inspire others.

Chapter 02

Problems I Faced

I Can't Express My Ideas

From the moment I decided to pave the way for how everyone, especially those my age, could become an author, I often found myself in moments of silence. Pen in hand, staring at empty pages, I struggled to express the ideas I had in my mind. What I mean here are the inspiring ideas—the ones that arrive unexpectedly and are often fleeting. It took me a long time to realise that anyone can generate such ideas by simply writing down whatever comes to mind and allowing their thoughts to flow.

In my journey toward becoming an author, I often felt stuck when trying to express my ideas on different book topics. There were countless moments of uncertainty where I found it difficult to settle on a specific subject to write about. At first, I explored various topics that intrigued me—different stories, themes, and experiences—but each time, I struggled to fully capture the essence of my thoughts. It felt as if I was constantly jumping from one idea to another, unable to fully commit to a single concept.

The challenge wasn't just about finding a topic; it was about finding the right words to express my thoughts clearly and in a way that would engage readers. Each idea seemed to need more development, and I felt like I was taking steps backwards rather than forward. This confusion and lack of clarity often made me question if I would ever be able to finish a book.

Eventually, I realised that my struggle to find a book topic was not an obstacle but rather a necessary part of the process. After experimenting with various subjects, I found a sense of clarity in writing about the very journey I was experiencing— becoming an author. This became my starting point. I realised that by writing about how I could become an author, I was not only finding my voice but also reflecting on my growth as a writer. It was a journey of self-discovery and realisation.

Once I had established the foundation of my first book, it was easier to branch out into other topics. Writing about the process of becoming an author allowed me to organise my thoughts and solidify my identity as a writer. From there, I could move on to explore other subjects that inspired me. The key to overcoming my initial frustration was acknowledging that writing about my own experience would serve as the starting point to explore other topics more deeply.

The process taught me that sometimes it's okay to start small. You don't have to figure everything out at once. By narrowing my focus to writing about becoming an author first, I found the structure and clarity I needed to move on to other topics that were meaningful to me. And now, with each new project, I approach it with more confidence and less self-doubt.

I Don't Have Enough Vocabulary

One of the biggest challenges I faced in my writing journey was the lack of a strong vocabulary, especially when writing in English. Growing up, I didn't feel confident in my language skills. English was not my first language, and the classes I attended were taught entirely in English. At first, I struggled to understand much of what was being said, let alone express myself in a meaningful way. This created a significant barrier for me in writing.

As I began to develop my ideas and attempt writing, I quickly realised how limited my vocabulary was. I felt frustrated and defeated because I couldn't find the right words to convey my thoughts. There was always a sense of incompleteness in my writing, as if I was unable to fully articulate what I was trying to say. It was disheartening to feel as though the wall of words that stood between me and the success I envisioned as an author was insurmountable.

Every time I sat down to write, I was reminded of how little I knew, and that constant feeling of inadequacy made me feel stuck. It was as though my ideas were trapped inside my mind, unable to find their way onto the page because I simply didn't have the words to express them. This limitation left me feeling sad and discouraged. I wanted to be a writer, but my vocabulary kept me from breaking through the barrier of creativity.

The sadness came from a deeper place, the feeling that I couldn't communicate my thoughts the way I wanted to. Writing, for me, was about sharing my ideas and connecting with others. Yet, without the proper vocabulary, it felt impossible to make that connection. I began to wonder if I would ever be able to write in a way that was clear, effective, and impactful.

Despite these struggles, I knew that if I wanted to succeed as a writer, I had to push through the frustration and find a way to improve. This was a turning point in my journey, where I realised that vocabulary wasn't just about knowing words, but about developing the ability to express myself in a meaningful way. I understood that the challenge I faced could be overcome, but it required dedication and consistent effort. It was then that I decided to focus on improving my vocabulary to break through the wall that was holding me back.

No One to Help?

Writing a book can often feel like a lonely journey, especially when you're doing it without a clear guide or mentor. In the beginning, I felt like I was completely on my own. There were moments when it seemed as though no one could help me. The pressure was overwhelming, particularly because of my age and the need for guidance in everything I was doing. It felt like I was expected to figure everything out by myself, without any direction.

I remember looking at my sister as she worked on her book. It seemed so effortless for her. And with every step she took, it felt like I was falling behind as if we were in some silent competition. This comparison, this constant feeling of being behind, added another layer of pressure that made everything seem so much harder.

I began to ask myself, "Why is this so hard for me? Why can't I seem to get it right? Why don't I have the support I need?" It felt like I was running a race that no one else could see, a race where I had no one to cheer me on or help me along the way. Watching others, including my sister, succeed only made the isolation worse. The uncertainty and the overwhelming pressure of trying to succeed on my own made the task seem even more impossible.

However, through this process, I came to an important realisation. While I may not have had anyone physically beside me every step of the way, I didn't have to face this challenge all alone. There were always ways to seek help, even if it wasn't immediately obvious. I started by taking matters into my own hands, writing down every idea that came to mind, even if I wasn't sure it would work. When I hit a wall or ran out of ideas, I turned to my family and teachers for feedback. I quickly learned that asking for help wasn't a sign of weakness or failure. In fact, it was a sign of growth and strength. Seeking feedback was one of the best ways to refine my ideas and improve my writing.

I also found valuable support through online writers' communities. These virtual spaces gave me the opportunity to connect with others who were going through similar struggles. They shared their stories, advice, and challenges, and I quickly realised that I wasn't the only one facing difficulties. These interactions helped me understand that, even when writing feels lonely, I wasn't truly alone in my journey. The encouragement I received from fellow writers was a lifeline, reminding me that it's okay to lean on others for support when the path feels unclear.

In the end, I learned an important lesson: Writing a book is a personal journey, but it doesn't have to be a solitary one. It's okay to feel pressure and doubt, but it's just as important to reach out for help when needed. Whether it's brainstorming ideas, getting feedback, or finding motivation, there are always people and resources available to help.

Now, as I share my story, I want to remind you that if you're feeling stuck, overwhelmed, or unsure about your writing, you don't have to carry that burden by yourself. If you're struggling with your plot, characters, or even how to structure your work, I am here to help. Writing can be a tough, long journey, but we don't have to go through it alone. Let's make the process easier, together.

Throughout my writing journey, I came to understand that writing a book is far from a smooth, easy path.

It's a journey filled with ups and downs, moments of doubt and frustration, but also moments of clarity and growth. Each challenge I faced along the way taught me something new, whether it was about myself, my writing, or the process itself. At times, I felt overwhelmed, questioning whether I was on the right track. But with every obstacle, I grew stronger. Each struggle, no matter how difficult, brought me closer to my goal of becoming an author.

Looking back, I realise that these challenges weren't setbacks but stepping stones. They forced me to improve my skills, expand my vocabulary, and push through moments of uncertainty. What once seemed impossible slowly became achievable. And though the road wasn't always easy, it was always worth it. Because at the end of the journey, I could look at my finished book and know that it was the product of persistence, hard work, and unwavering determination.

If you're facing similar difficulties in your writing journey, I want you to know that you are not alone. Writing is a process that takes time, patience, and perseverance. There will be moments of doubt, but remember, those moments don't define you. Keep going, even when it feels hard. With each word, each sentence, and each page, you're moving closer to your dream.

Everyone's journey is unique, but one thing remains constant: It's always worth it in the end. So, if you're struggling or feeling stuck, know that the challenges you face today will only make your success even sweeter. Keep writing, keep learning, and keep believing in yourself. You can do it.

How I Became an Author

As I mentioned, it took me a year and a half to reach the first draft of my book and truly understand the life cycle of publishing. One whole year of that time was spent overcoming the challenges and problems that kept me from becoming an author. The rest of the time was dedicated to outlining a clear path forward for anyone who aspires to write a book. After all the struggles, I realised that the process of writing and publishing doesn't have to be complicated. I want to make it as clear and straightforward as possible, similar to how artificial intelligence works.

Take your First Step and Leave your Print

I'm not a shy girl, but I also tend not to speak much. This might explain a lot about my behaviour. What I discovered, though, was that writing offered me a unique way to express myself—a space where I could take my time and say exactly what I wanted. This time, it was mine. Writing became my escape, my safe space where I could communicate on my terms, free from the pressure of speaking quickly or worrying about how I might be perceived.

Writing isn't always easy, and there were countless times when I struggled with focus and motivation. At times, the journey to becoming an author felt endless. The obstacles seemed overwhelming, and I wondered if I would ever be able to finish my book. But over time, I realised that the key to overcoming these challenges wasn't to try to solve everything at once; it was to tackle them one by one. By breaking down the obstacles and solving them step by step, I was able to make progress, even when things felt impossible.

In this chapter, I want to share the solutions that helped me stay focused and move forward on my journey to becoming an author. Everyone's writing process is different, and there is no one-size-fits-all path. However, I found that addressing these problems helped me overcome the challenges that arose and get closer to my goal of becoming an author.

I took the first step, and what I found is that writing is like a fingerprint or an iris print—unique to every individual. Each writer's journey is different; each story has its own path. What works for one person may not work for another. There's no perfect formula for becoming an author. It's about finding your own way, your own voice, and your own mark.

That's what I wanted to do: leave my own print on the page. Just as no two fingerprints are the same, no two writing journeys are either. And I knew that in order to succeed, I had to embrace my uniqueness and trust my process. Every word I wrote, and every challenge I faced helped me build my own path forward.

And from here, I ask everyone to put their own "pages print" out into the world. Share your unique story, express your ideas, and inspire others in your own way. Just as my journey helped me find my voice, so can yours. Whether it's through writing, speaking, or any other form of expression, every individual has something valuable to share. Let's inspire others by embracing our uniqueness and showing them the many ways we can all leave our mark.

Be Close to Your Environment

One of the first lessons I learned was how important it is to be in the right environment. Nature has a special way of calming the mind and sparking creativity. I still remember the first writing idea that came to my mind—it was inspired by the sight of clouds forming in the sky. I imagined them as creatures, silently communicating with each other. That image stuck with me, and it made me realise how powerful it was to be in a place that made me feel more connected to the world around me.

Certain places have a unique way of awakening creativity. I recall the quiet beaches in Malaysia, where the sound of gentle waves against the shore seemed to clear my mind and open it up to new ideas. I also found peace in the forests of Malaysia, where the rustling of leaves and the calming stillness of the trees allowed me to focus. Even the mountaintops in Oman brought a sense of clarity, as if I was closer to both the world and myself. The River Nile in Sudan was another place that inspired me deeply. All of these places I have physically visited, both during and after writing this book, helped me feel grounded and constantly enriched my first book, nurturing my creativity.

However, it's crucial to recognise that the environment is not only about nature. My interactions with social life and my understanding of the situation in my country also played significant roles in shaping how I saw the world and, ultimately, how I wrote. Life's circumstances, the relationships I built, and even the challenges I faced, all influenced my perspective. My environment, both natural and social, helped me see things in a mature way, giving me the insights I needed to understand not only the world around me but also myself.

Nature taught me that inspiration is all around us—sometimes, we just need to step outside to find it. Whether it's the beauty of a quiet beach, the serenity of a forest, the grandeur of a mountaintop, or the peaceful flow of a river, nature offers countless ways to connect with our inner creativity. For me, being in these places wasn't just about escaping the noise of everyday life; it was about immersing myself in environments that nurtured my imagination and gave me the space to reflect and write.

It's also important to mention that the long writing exercises at my school served as starting points for many of the ideas in my book. These exercises gave me the opportunity to develop my writing, and with more time, I realised I just needed to express myself in more detail. All of these experiences, both in nature and in school, helped me to hone my writing and shaped my journey as an author.

Organise Your Ideas

Writing isn't just about creating a book for me; it extends to every form of writing, whether it's for school English exercises, speeches, essays, or any other subject. I've been familiar with English from an early age, having participated in language clubs and speeches starting in Grade 3. At the beginning of my writing journey, I often found my ideas scattered and disorganised. It was difficult to form a cohesive narrative or argument, and I realised that the key to making my writing meaningful was learning how to organise my thoughts properly.

I soon discovered that the first step to effective writing is organising your ideas. It wasn't just about sitting down to write; it was about setting up a structure that would allow my thoughts to flow smoothly. I needed to give my ideas a clear direction and purpose. This meant breaking down my ideas into manageable pieces and figuring out how each thought connected to the next.

At first, it was challenging. I would have a jumble of ideas but no clear way to make them all fit together.

However, I soon realised that organising my thoughts was the foundation for writing a meaningful piece, whether it was for a book or a school assignment. I needed to focus on making my thoughts clear and objective so that my writing would make sense to my readers.

I started using outlines, brainstorming sessions, and simple notes to break down my ideas before I began writing. This helped me identify the main points I wanted to discuss and allowed me to map out the logical flow of my arguments or narrative.

Organising my ideas this way didn't just help with my book; it also improved my English writing exercises in other subjects.

Over time, I learned how important it was for each idea to lead logically into the next. This structure helped create a story or argument that was not only easy to follow but also engaging for my readers. The process of organising my time and ideas became an essential tool for every piece of writing I worked on, helping me stay focused, coherent, and productive.

Organise Your Time

"You should submit the homework tomorrow" is a phrase I often heard from teachers, and they would repeat it frequently. I've always been committed to my duties, even without explicit instructions.

Growing up, I learned from my parents that this sense of responsibility was part of time management. At first, it felt overwhelming, but over time, I started to understand the importance of having a schedule, a timetable, and other concepts related to managing time. I realised that organising my time effectively was key to achieving my goals. My parents reinforced this idea by echoing the same instructions I received from teachers at home. Their guidance aimed to help me achieve the best results, both in school and in life.

Time management became a significant challenge when school resumed. During the break, I had plenty of time to write, but once classes started again, I found myself overwhelmed with schoolwork and daily tasks. Balancing writing with my academic responsibilities was tough. However, I quickly realised that I needed to find a way to manage my time efficiently.

I decided to set weekends aside for writing. This dedicated time allowed me to reflect on my progress and continue working on my book without the distraction of school assignments. I also sought guidance from a teacher, who offered helpful feedback and advice, helping me make the most of the limited time I had for writing. By organising my time this way, I was able to stay on track with both my studies and my creative work.

Increase Your Language Skills

A common question I am often asked is, "Medad, is English your first or second language?" Regardless of the answer, I believe it's important to take this moment to clarify something crucial: writing, for me, is not tied to the English language alone. The ability to express ideas effectively can be done in any language. However, here, I want to focus specifically on writing in English and how improving language skills in this area is essential for expressing complex thoughts and ideas, especially when it comes to writing books and becoming an author

For me, writing in English presented a challenge. I initially felt unsure of my vocabulary and worried that my words wouldn't fully capture the depth of my thoughts. Given the potential global reach of my writing, with the possibility of millions of people seeing it, I felt an even greater pressure to get it right. While the outcome of my book's reach was uncertain, I knew I had to prepare for the possibility of it reaching a wider audience. I realised that to grow as a writer, I needed to build my language skills to express myself with greater precision and clarity.

Improving my English language skills became a top priority. I committed myself to daily practice— speaking with others, watching educational videos, listening to speeches, and reading books. These activities didn't just expand my vocabulary but also enhanced my understanding of sentence structures, tone, and nuances of the language. As I practised, I became more fluent and more confident in expressing myself. With time, I started to feel more comfortable using English to articulate my thoughts, and this made me feel like I was finding my true voice as a writer.

In writing, language is the vehicle that carries our ideas. The more we improve it, the better we can share our messages with the world. Through my journey of learning and practising English, I was able to overcome my initial struggles and develop a stronger, more confident approach to writing. And it wasn't just about expanding my vocabulary; it was about refining my ability to communicate effectively, clearly, and creatively.

Enhance and Develop Your Vocabulary

At home, there was a friendly competition between my sister and me. We would randomly collect words and try to figure out their meanings. Was it enough to know the word and its definition to satisfy the idea of vocabulary? Initially, I thought so. I believed that knowing the word and its meaning was enough to consider it part of my vocabulary. However, I soon came to realise that a strong vocabulary is much more than just memorising definitions; it's a vital skill for effective communication.

I quickly understood how critical a rich vocabulary was to my growth as a writer. Before I grasped the true importance of expanding my vocabulary, I often found it challenging to express myself fully. My thoughts would feel limited, and I couldn't always find the right words to capture my ideas. But as I began to pay closer attention to new words in books, speeches, and conversations, I noticed my vocabulary starting to grow.

I made a conscious effort to learn new words daily. Whenever I encountered unfamiliar terms, I would look up their meanings, use them in sentences, and practice incorporating them into my writing and speech. I also joined groups where I could actively use these new words in conversations, which helped me reinforce my learning and gain confidence. Over time, this practice not only expanded my vocabulary but also made it easier for me to express myself more creatively and clearly.

A rich vocabulary allowed me to communicate my ideas with greater precision and flair. It gave me the freedom to choose from a wider range of words to convey emotions, describe scenes, or explain concepts more effectively. Developing a strong vocabulary has been a key part of my journey as a writer, and I continue to value the importance of learning new words every day.

Develop Your Writing Skills

Improving my writing was not an overnight transformation but rather a gradual process that took time, dedication, and constant effort. When I first began, I didn't have a clear understanding of how to structure my writing, or how to maintain a focused narrative. My thoughts often felt scattered, and the flow of my ideas was not always as clear as I wanted it to be. But I was determined to improve.

One of the most important things I learned was the necessity of consistent practice. I realised that writing is a skill that needs to be nurtured every day, just like any other craft. So, I wrote regularly, whether it was short stories, journal entries, or notes for my book. This practice helped me sharpen my skills and develop a routine.

Reading also played a significant role in my growth as a writer. The more I read, the more I learned about different writing styles, structures, and how to convey ideas effectively. I paid attention to how authors built their narratives, how they developed their characters, and how they made their writing engaging. Reading gave me new perspectives on how to approach my own writing and helped me refine my voice.

However, perhaps the most influential factor in my development was the feedback I received from my

English teacher. She became an incredible mentor in my journey. She was not just a teacher but also a guide who helped me navigate the complexities of writing. She patiently reviewed my work and pointed out areas where I could improve, offering valuable suggestions to enhance clarity and structure. Her advice was always constructive, helping me take my writing to the next level.

Through her mentorship, I learned how to focus my ideas more effectively and how to express them clearly. She also helped me find my own unique writing style, one that felt true to my voice. Her guidance made me more confident in my abilities and encouraged me to keep pushing forward, even when I faced challenges or self-doubt.

With time, I began to see progress. My writing became more organised, my ideas flowed more naturally, and I found it easier to express myself clearly. What had once been a struggle was now something I could do with confidence. Writing had evolved from something daunting into something I genuinely enjoyed.

Improving my writing skills was not a quick fix but a journey that required persistence, practice, and mentorship. With each step, I grew as a writer, learning not only technical skills but also how to express myself more authentically. As I continued to develop, I became more confident in my ability to communicate my ideas effectively, knowing that writing is a skill that can always be improved with dedication and the right support.

Find Your Areas of Interest

Finding areas of interest for writing was not easy, especially in the early stages of my journey. When I started out, I didn't know exactly what topics would inspire me to write a book. But as I became more immersed in my environment, many ideas began to surface. I started to realise that writing about something you truly care about is key to creating meaningful work.

To find my areas of interest, I took time to reflect on the things that truly excited me, my hobbies, activities, and experiences that sparked a sense of passion. I asked

myself what topics I enjoyed talking about, reading about, or learning more about. This reflection helped me gain insight into what mattered most to me.

I also revisited past projects and looked back at topics that had captured my attention in the past. Those projects served as clues to my deeper interests, helping me to identify patterns in the types of things I enjoyed writing about.

Additionally, I made an effort to step out of my comfort zone and experiment with new activities. Trying new things and exploring different perspectives helped me uncover fresh areas of interest that I hadn't considered before.

Ultimately, these discoveries played a significant role in shaping my writing. Writing about things I cared about made my work more authentic and meaningful, and it kept me motivated through the challenges. Finding my areas of interest allowed me to connect with my audience more deeply, and it has been a guiding principle in my writing journey.

Develop Your Book Idea

Becoming an author of a book was not something I decided overnight. It was a gradual process that started with just one line, one idea, and a lot of uncertainty. In the beginning, I had no clear vision of what my book would be about. I often found myself doubting my abilities and feeling unsure of the direction I wanted to take. Every time I tried to develop a concept, I felt like I was hitting a wall.

However, the more I wrote down my thoughts and ideas, the more my vision began to take shape. I learned that it's normal to feel unclear at the start and that the key is to keep writing. As I explored different topics and considered various possibilities, I started to see connections and patterns in my thoughts. The more ideas I jotted down, the more clarity I gained. I came to understand that this process wasn't about getting everything perfect right away but about allowing my ideas to evolve over time.

As I continued to refine my thoughts, I eventually had a clear, well-defined concept for my book. This clarity became my guiding light, giving me a sense of purpose and direction. Once I had that solid idea, I was ready to take the next step: reaching out to professionals in the book industry.

I knew that in order to bring my book to life, I would need expert guidance. So, my parents began contacting professionals—writers, editors, and agents, who could help me transform my concept into a finished work. This step was crucial, as it allowed me to connect with people who could offer valuable advice and support throughout the writing and publishing process.

Looking back, I can see how important it was to keep pushing forward, even when I felt uncertain. Each step, from writing down a single idea to contacting experts in the field, was part of the journey toward becoming an author. Today, I realise that having a clear idea for your book is critical, but equally important is the persistence and willingness to explore, refine, and seek guidance along the way.

Write Your First Draft

Writing the first draft of my book was a monumental moment in my journey as a writer. Before I put pen to paper or fingers to keyboard, I had countless doubts. Could I really write a whole book? Would my ideas make sense? Was I good enough? But I knew one thing: I had to start somewhere.

The first draft wasn't about perfection; it was about creation. I gave myself permission to write a rough, unpolished version of my thoughts. It didn't need to be flawless. I just needed to get my ideas down. There was something incredibly freeing about that. I stopped focusing on making every sentence perfect and allowed myself to write freely, knowing that I would have plenty of time to refine things later.

At first, the words didn't flow easily. There were days when I struggled to put my ideas into sentences, and I felt frustrated. But little by little, I began to see my vision take shape. The first draft wasn't about achieving greatness immediately; it was about building the foundation for something bigger.

The more I wrote, the more confident I became. I realised that the first draft wasn't the end but the beginning of the journey. It was a rough sketch of what the final product could be. With each word I added, my ideas grew stronger, and my understanding of the story and message I wanted to share deepened.

When I finally completed the first draft, it felt like a huge accomplishment. I named it my "First Book Draft," not because it was finished but because it marked the first real step toward becoming an author.

It was proof that I had taken my ideas from my mind and transformed them into something tangible. That first draft was my foundation, a place to build from.

I learned that writing a first draft is an essential part of the writing process. It doesn't need to be perfect, and it doesn't need to be polished. What matters most is that it exists, that it lays the groundwork for the next stages of refinement. The confidence to write the first draft came from understanding this: it was just a start, and everything else would follow. And with that, I had taken my first true step toward becoming an author.

Chapter 04

The New Things Became My Print

4.1   New Things

When I started writing my book, I decided to include a section called "New Things," not because these things were unusual, but because they were unfamiliar to people my age. To truly understand them, one needs to step into the world of adults and professionals. Even the term "professional" was new to me when I first began.

The most significant shift in my writing journey occurred after completing Chapter 3, where I focused on encouraging others my age to get into writing. It made me realise how important it was to ensure that my work would be recognised as *mine* and not claimed by someone else.

Around this time, people began talking about ISBN, and at first, I was just as confused as anyone else. I didn't know what it stood for or how it was relevant. But eventually, I learned that ISBN stands for *International Standard Book Number*. It's a vital tool for securing the copyright of your book and making sure it is recognised internationally. An ISBN allows your book to be listed in public libraries, whether it's in print or digital form.

In the beginning, understanding these new concepts was difficult. Even learning how to pronounce certain words correctly was challenging. Thankfully, my

English teacher from India helped me through this journey. She simplified complex ideas and acted more like a coach, guiding me through the process rather than just teaching me facts.

Now, I'm at the stage where I'm ready to apply for my own ISBN through a publisher. By signing an agreement, I will ensure my rights are protected, and the publisher will assist with distribution and publishing. Reaching this milestone has brought me immense joy. To me, it feels like the final step on the path to becoming an author—sharing ideas that can improve people's lives and contribute something valuable to the world.

4.2   Eye Print, Fingerprint, and ISBN

One of the new things that caught my attention, and I found both interesting and a bit amusing, was how the lines in the ISBN logo resemble those of a fingerprint. While their patterns and alignments are different, they have a certain similarity. It's almost as if your fingerprint is placed before you, marking the uniqueness of your work. Just like your fingerprint identifies you, the ISBN identifies your book, making sure no one else can claim it as theirs. It's a powerful reminder that just as you leave your fingerprint on the world, your work can leave an imprint that helps others and makes a difference.

I also discovered something called eye prints, which are even more intricate than fingerprints. During my research, I found websites that let you take an eye print, but they charge a fee, usually around $70. This process reminded me of the work involved in publishing a book and acquiring an ISBN. Just like your eye print, you need to pay for this "print" to secure your work and make it uniquely yours.

This chapter made me feel proud because it meant I was getting close to completing the writing process. Now, I fully understand how everything connects. I encourage everyone reading this to leave your print on the world today, not tomorrow - just keep going.

Many of you might wonder, "How can a girl who's only nine years old understand all of this and explain such complex ideas?" The answer is simple: I'm sharing what I've learned from my research. In the end, I discovered that knowledge is all around us. It's easy to understand once you know where to look. The real challenge is not the new things themselves; it's the determination to keep going, the desire to connect the dots, and the persistence to understand everything clearly. It took me months to learn all of this, but it wasn't the new information that was difficult. It was about understanding and connecting everything together in a way that made sense.

Chapter 05

Marketing and Sales

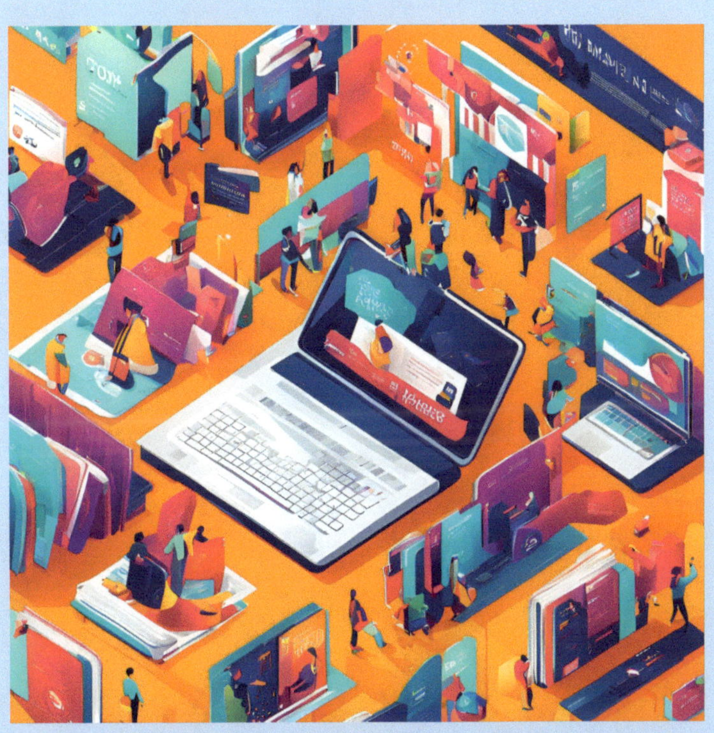

Amazon Also is Here

I would like to share my short story about the marketing and sale of my book. At first, when I went online and discovered Amazon, I only knew it as a platform for online shopping. I didn't realise that Amazon also sells authors' books. Of course, this was a normal realisation for me, as I'm new to the world of writing as a very young girl. It didn't take me long to understand this since I was already familiar with shopping and being aware of the prices of things I regularly buy.

So, discovering that I could sell my book on Amazon made me very happy. The idea that my book could reach people and I could become known was exciting. It even sparked a fun competition between me and my sister, where we challenged each other to finish our books and post them on Amazon or other platforms to see who could become famous first.

I'll try to explain what I discovered during my research at this stage of my book. Once your book is accredited, there are a few important steps to consider. First, you need to decide how to publish it:

- Hard copy Books: These are books that are printed only when someone orders them, helping to reduce costs and inventory.
- E-books: Digital versions of your book that can be sold and downloaded online, to be available to readers worldwide.

— Audiobooks: You can also choose to publish your book in audio format, reaching those who prefer listening to books rather than reading them.

Understanding these options helped me decide what would work best for my book, and I realised that there are many ways to get my ideas out to the world.

The most difficult part for me was reading and understanding the agreement with the publisher and distributor that was recommended by my father. The agreement was long and detailed, covering terms related to marketing and the sale of my book.

My journey through this process felt like it took days to fully understand the entire cycle, from agreeing with the distributor and agent to receiving feedback from readers. It wasn't an easy process, but it was worth it as I gained a deeper understanding of how the publishing world works.

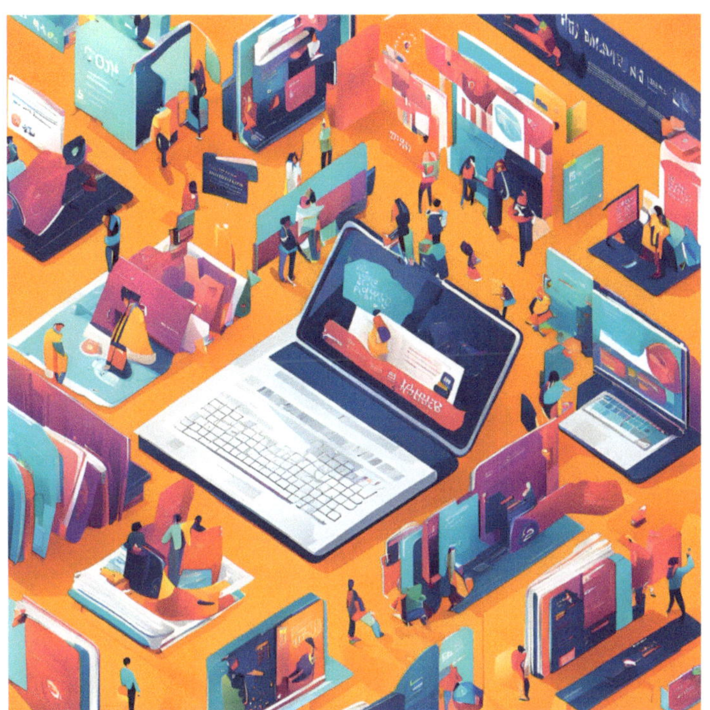

Chapter 06

To-Dos

Write for Yourself First

I want to share something important with people of my age and others as well. The lessons I've learned, and the milestones I've reached may resonate with you. There were very important moments along the way that I should mention—things I learned from my parents and close advisers who patiently guided me. People like my teachers and others who gave me advice without expecting anything in return. They simply wanted to see me succeed.

One of the most crucial pieces of advice I received was from those around me: buy a new notebook and pen. This was something that would stay in my memory as I started writing what I truly felt, liked, and desired, almost like starting a personal diary. The act of writing things down was an important first step for me. I also bought a laptop, which helped me develop faster computer skills, especially using tools like Word. More importantly, it connected me to the professional world beyond just my phone. It was like opening the door to endless possibilities for learning, connecting, and growing.

Looking back, maybe everything I've gone through in the chapters of my book won't match the thoughts or ideas of others. My experiences are unique to me, and that's okay. But the key takeaway is this: take a pen and notebook and write down what you truly feel and want. It's not about following someone else's path; it's about following your own.

You might wonder, how did a girl like me accept all these challenges for over a year and a half, just to finalise the first draft of this book? How did I keep going, even when things felt overwhelming? The answer is simple. Even if what I've mentioned might seem insignificant or meaningless to some, the most important thing is to start thinking about how you can leave your own mark on the world. Don't feel pressured to follow someone else's pace or goals. Don't force yourself unless you truly feel it inside. Find what drives you, and let that be your motivation.

I'll never forget the moment when I looked up at the clouds and felt inspired. It was like something clicked inside me, and I knew I had to write what truly matched who I am and what I was feeling. That moment reminded me of something very important: when you write, do it first for yourself. It's not just about putting words on a page; it's about expressing your true self. You should write in a way that resonates with your own emotions and experiences.

As I looked at the clouds, I realised that writing is not just a way to communicate with others, but a way to connect with yourself. And from that connection, you can imagine how your words might inspire others—

especially people my age. Writing can be a bridge that links your thoughts and feelings with the world around you.

I can now encapsulate everything I've experienced through what I've learned. For me, the key is this: when you write, let it come from a place of honesty. Write what feels right for you, and think about how it might touch others. It's not about trying to impress or fit in; it's about sharing something real, something that reflects who you are.

Writing is an act of vulnerability, an opportunity to express the deepest parts of yourself. It's about connecting with others through your truth, not through trying to be someone you're not. As I've gone through this journey, I've realised that being authentic is the most important thing you can do with your words. When you let go of the pressure to conform and instead focus on what matters most to you, that's when your voice truly shines.

I also encourage anyone who wants to write to do so with an open heart. Don't be afraid to share your story, your feelings, and your ideas. Let your words be a reflection of who you are, and trust that they will find a place in the hearts of others. Because in the end, it's not about impressing anyone; it's about being real, being true, and leaving a mark that is uniquely yours.

The End

At the end of my book, I want to express just how proud I am of myself and how truly happy I feel for what I've accomplished.

In the end, that's exactly what I did. I followed my own path, staying true to what I believed in, and now I'm proud of myself for adding something of value to people's lives. My book will live with them forever, and the knowledge I've shared will remain even after I'm gone. Knowledge has the power to endure, and that's something to be proud of.

Looking back at this journey, I realise that every step, every challenge, and every moment of doubt brought me closer to where I am today. Writing this book wasn't just about finishing a project; it was about discovering my own voice and sharing it with the world, I've learned so much along the way, and I can't wait to see how this book touches others and inspires them.

So, as I close this chapter, I can say with confidence that I'm proud of what I've created. It's a part of me, and it will continue to live on, making a difference, just as I hope to.

Finally, my name is Medad, which means "ink" in Arabic. Just like ink flows from a pen to create words, my thoughts and stories flow onto these pages, leaving a mark of my own. And just as ink endures on paper, the knowledge and messages I've shared through my writing will live on, hopefully making a difference for others.